MW01709054

PLAIN VANILLA JESUS

A True Story About Plain Vanilla

By
Pastor Marie Sorrentino

PLAIN VANILLA JESUS

Contact the author at:
plainvanillajesus@yahoo.com

ISBN: 1-59352-047-6

Published by:
Christian Services Network
1975 Janich Ranch Ct.
El Cajon, CA 92019
Toll Free: 1-866-484-6184

All Scriptures are taken from The Amplified Bible unless otherwise indicated.

Printed in the United States of America

What Others Are Saying

Real... That is the only way to describe *Plain Vanilla Jesus*. People who are searching for answers in life through many other sources, will find Jesus through this book. You will love the way Marie shares her own stories. You will laugh... you will cry... you will see Jesus as you have never seen Him before.

Pastors Paul & Carolyn Tebbano
Harvest Church, Clifton Park, NJ

This is a miraculous story of what God can do when two most unlikely people become fully yielded to God. I know *Plain Vanilla Jesus* to be true. I was there in New York when much of it occurred. This book will strengthen your faith to believe God and to see the impossible and the improbable happen in your life. It's a faith builder – you need to read it.

Benjamin J. Crandall
Chancellor
Zion Bible College

Get ready to re-evaluate your relationship with Christ through this realistic look at how God can take a life and make it right! Through Pastor Marie's story you will see that God is real and furthermore that God is no respector of persons. What He's done for this small but great spiritual giant, He'll do for all of us who will receive. You will laugh and shout, put your hands to your head and your heart; and most of all, you will want to know more about the Jesus that set Marie free and made her whole. Read *Plain Vanilla Jesus* and get a glimpse of God's goodness!

Bishop Isaiah S. Williams Jr.
Miami, FL
Jesus People Ministries

Table of Contents

FOREWORD

Theresa and I have known the Sorrentinos now for well over 20 years.

Plain Vanilla Jesus is the story of the grace, the love, the tenderness and – last but not least – the Power of God at work in the life of a dear saint of God.

The Bible says:

> *You have not chosen me, but I have chosen you...*
> (John 15:16a)

As you read this marvelous story, this scripture will come to you over and over again.

Marie is a special chosen vessel for God's purposes.

> *Laugh, cry, rejoice with her through the true story of Plain Vanilla Jesus. This was the Lord's doing, and it is marvelous in our eyes.*
> (Mark 12:11)

Thank you, Marie, for showing us how God can take us just as we are–and pour His love through us.

God's Servant,
Morris Cerullo

The Author Thanks ...

Thank you, New Covenant Tabernacle, our very special church. It would take forever to tell you how much I love all of you, even though you have made me so crazy. NCT has truly been a hospital for Jesus.

Lily of the Valley family, your hands have been Christ's hands. You have loved the unlovely. Jesus didn't look like the Catholic portrait of Him with big blue eyes, blonde hair and a perfect nose. On the contrary, He was a Jew with a pretty big–sized nose that breathed the breath of life that He shared with you and me.

To my dear husband, John, let me say thank you for being a shepherd and not a hireling. Thank you for not being jealous when I fed the whole world and sometimes served you the leftovers. Thank you for sharing me with everyone. Thank you for always letting me put Jesus first. It's okay that you prefer chocolate to vanilla. That's what makes our life so special together. That's what makes the balance, which is the key to life.

Father, thank You for sending Jesus. There would be no book without Your Book of Life. And thank You for making chickens. With Your anointing, my soup has healed hundreds.

Jesus, thank You for dying for me and searching me out, so that I could talk about You.

Holy Spirit, Gentle Dove, thank You for always revealing Jesus so I could know His will. Thank You for putting up with us, trying to answer all our questions and working out the wrinkles and spots in this Italian couple. You truly have the right name, The Comforter.

To God and God alone be the glory, as with much love I present this book,

Your daughter,
Marie

A NOTE ...

A special thanks to Wilsie–secretary, writer, bathroom cleaner, accountant, bottle washer, gift wrapper, our memory bank, our speller, our organizer and great encourager ... but most of all, a friend. Thank God for the excess lines on her brain; she was able to fill the lack of lines on mine to put this book together with much love and patience. Thank you for loving Jesus enough to love me.

Your Sister and Pastor,
Marie

Introduction

This book is long overdue, so bear with me if the meat is a little overcooked. If you are a reader that likes to look up big words in your dictionary, you have chosen the wrong book. Why? Because *Plain Vanilla Jesus* is a true story about plain vanilla–not a sundae with marshmallows and any of those fancy ice cream flavors that are available now. Back during the times that I have written about, the only flavor choices we had were vanilla and chocolate and maybe strawberry. So you couldn't get confused if you just chose plain vanilla (even though John and I could have added nuts to ours, since that is what our life was like at first).

You will laugh, you will cry, and you may not even want to finish this book. But please do! The latter is greater than the beginning.

Chapter 1

Where Do I Start?

Okay, where do I start?! I guess back in Brooklyn, New York, where it all began. In those days no one cared for a title; they just wanted to be the toughest–these were the 50's.

Every area of the city really had no visible dividing line that you could see, but each was separate anyway because the people made sure of that. There were the Italians like my family, the Jews, the Puerto Ricans, the Blacks, the Irish, and a small section of Norwegians and Swedes. The Italians were the strongest–no doubt because of all the food they were always eating.

All the windows and doors were open in those days. You did not hear any gun shots from houses. The only loud noise was gas from all the garlic the people ate. As you sat on your step outside, you could always smell what the people were cooking, especially my Mom. She was the best Italian cook.

You did not buy food by the week then. Who could afford that? We ran around the corner every day to buy something to cook for dinner. Mom learned how to take anything and make a meal out of it. Whatever we were having, there was always a piece of fresh Italian bread to go with it–then your jaws were in business.

Mom grew up with 18 brothers and three sisters, although one sister was run over by a horse and died when she was 13. That's 21 children all together in one family. So, as you can see, she was used to having a lot of mouths to feed.

Three years older than me, my only sister was the gem of my life. Her name was Carolyn and she was born with scoliosis, a condition of the spine which formed a very large hunchback on her body. She was very beautiful and very smart. I was just the opposite. I have, all in all, about a 6th grade level of education.

In those days, if you had any deformity or anything physically wrong with you, you would be put in what was called the "hammer and nails" class at school. This was basically a class for the mentally retarded, but anyone with a physical disability was set apart and sent there.

Mom came to school, pinned the principal to the wall and said, "You are giving my daughter an opportunity to use her brain, not her body. If she does not perform, you can put her back in that class. But Carolyn is getting a fair chance to prove herself!"

Mom was tough. She had a perseverance that would not quit. The school did not like people who had any physical problems, especially one that was so obvious, because they said it might upset and disturb the other children. I thank the Lord that even then He was with us. Carolyn went all through school and graduated with the highest honors and with much favor. Even years later, her teachers corresponded with her.

Mom's Parents

My Family

Dad's Family

Marie at 3 years old

Mom and Dad

Mom was a seamstress, always sewing even when there seemed like there was nothing available to use for material. She would take down the curtains and make blouses for us or little doll dresses for our dolls. And that was the only time she sat down. Nobody sat down in our house. We all had to keep busy. Our house did not have much furniture but it was spotless.

In Brooklyn when you hung your clothes on the line, there would always be an unspoken contest to see whose clothing was the whitest. The women checked to see if there were any socks that were not neatly mended. It also counted how straight and neatly you draped the clothes one to the other on the line. Hey, these women washed on those wash boards for hours, using all that bluing to make them white! Why shouldn't they have a contest? After all, just pressing a shirt or sewing on a button today is no great accomplishment when you look back to those days.

Dad was a barber. One of eight boys, he was studying to become a priest and preparing to go to Italy. His family gave him a farewell party and there he met Mom. She was the first woman in his life and he married her.

The times were hard but very plain vanilla–simple. There was never confusion. It was yes or no, black or white. In the world we live in today, there is nothing but confusion, because the devil is the author of it.

My family didn't have a personal relationship with Jesus Christ but we did have religion. We were Catholic and Sunday was a day set aside for Mass. Even the stores honored the Sabbath and they were all closed on Sundays. How sad! Today there is very little respect shown for the Lord's day.

Growing up in the streets of Brooklyn was like living in another nation. Brooklyn and New York City were two different places. New York City was everything thrown together in mass confusion, but Brooklyn was very orderly. Even now in Brooklyn many people still live in the same house or apartment they have been in for fifty years and they still have the same telephone number.

Okay, back to me. In school I spent most of my time inside the wardrobes where the coats were hung up because everyone's lunch was there and I always wanted to know what everyone else was eating. There were pepper and eggs, meatballs, sausage sandwiches, all left over with Sunday's sauce. Yes, I ended up in the principal's office, with a lot of tomato sauce on my face and loving it.

But Mom did not, and discipline was as thick as a good sauce in those days. Too bad they do not know how to apply it today–it really works! But I guess they give five to 10 years in jail for child abuse now. Many times this happens because of the inability to apply discipline with love. The Word says a child left to himself will bring much shame to his parents. That is what America is experiencing today.

I chose all the wrong people to hang out with in school, thinking in some way that I would protect my sister. Meanwhile Carolyn went with all the right people and never had a fight. She wore a huge brace around her body. My heart would break when people made fun of her. She did not know it and neither did I, but she was my best friend until I met Jesus.

(Now don't get bored with me! Just keep reading. This story is like an antipasto. It has a little bit of everything in it and you cannot leave out anything because it just will not taste right.)

Now it is 1955 and I'm in the seventh grade. I admit I would not have gotten that far if I hadn't sat by that smart kid and cheated by looking at all her tests. I'm 13 years old, five feet tall, weighing 98 lbs., with long black hair–a cute Italian as far as the guys could see and say.

I'm 13, so I'm supposed to be a little rebellious. Mine was not a Christian life at this age, although I was living a moral life. Just being moral does not make you a miracle–but usually it does make you a mess, because the life of Christ is not a moral life but a sanctified one. A life changed by God is a life willing to obey, not because of something taught to your head, but to your heart.

The most I ever knew about sex was having a mother who was very concerned about us sitting on a dirty toilet. When I asked her one day how you got pregnant, her reply to me was, "Just don't sit on a dirty toilet." From that day on, that was my thinking pattern, so I stood over toilets to urinate and had no problems.

I joined a so–called gang called the "Hawks." Nobody really could afford a black leather jacket in those days and if you went out with one of these guys, you got to wear their motorcycle jacket.

Do you remember Fonzie from the television show Happy Days? He was so different from the clean cut kids, with his leather jacket and motorcycle. That show is nostalgia, not reality. In the 50's, people like him were rebels. They didn't fit into the regular crowd and didn't want to. I just wanted to fit in somewhere and it didn't seem wrong to me at the time. Usually only one girl in the group was willing to lay down and the rest of us just liked to tease, not to please.

Red M&Ms candies were my lipstick. Who could afford lipstick or the beating for wearing it? You never told the truth to Mom, and eventually you justified all your lies.

CHAPTER 2

Girl Meets Boy

Okay, okay, John! We are coming to you now! There he was–a good looking, muscle-bound Italian–5' 7," but to me he looked six feet tall! There are no Goliaths among Italians. I guess all the food goes to their sides, not the top of their heads. Who cared! He still seemed the tallest one to me. But of course at that time he only knew my name. We met because his girlfriend at the time was my friend. I was 13 and he was 16.

I am going to jump quickly over ages 14 to 19 in my life, because during those years John had many girlfriends, and I was not one of them. His way of life and his self-assured attitude–having no problem knowing who he was–were just too much for me to handle. He never asked me out anyway. But that doesn't mean I didn't keep track of him. Oh, he was so cute!

John went from being a black belt in karate to posing for the centerfold in the *Body Beautiful* magazine to receiving two scholarships to college for football. He was a New York state championship swimmer at 14 years old, swimming in the ocean at Coney Island in zero–degree water in the middle of the winter in the Iceberg Club. He dove out of airplanes, landing in trees, and he drove fancy cars.

Finally he received his so–called "calling" by his family in the Mafia. John came from a strong, Mafia–related family. His mother was only 4' 8" but you never messed with her. His father was a great provider and was in the furniture business.

Personally I found that all so boring, since my life was filled with Eggplant Parmesan and every exotic Italian food dish that turned me on. Thank God I never got fat.

I became a hair dresser at 14 years of age, and, without a license, I was able to smuggle myself into a shop to help and I learned so much. These were the years when hair was teased so high that the Italian guys did not have a chance in size. The girls were definitely taller.

Hair spray had definitely made a hole, not only through the ozone layer, but right through to Mars. Bobbie pins could have built a prison from one end of the United States to the other. The rollers we used were so big you needed a chiropractor for six months after just one night's sleep with them on your head. There was no limit to the cost of beauty. And everyone seemed to look the same.

Now, I cannot imagine my life without Christ. Beauty is your beast without Christ reflecting through you. And your hair is just a fur ball unless you know that He has the hairs on your head numbered. So let's return to the days of my life.

There was no one who worked harder than I did. There were no eight hour days either. It was very common for me to work from 8 in the morning until midnight. Girls were lined up for hours to get their hair done. I weighed 102 lbs. and was ready to collapse.

John at 17 years old

Marie at 13 years old

Dating

John as a body builder

John at 18 years old

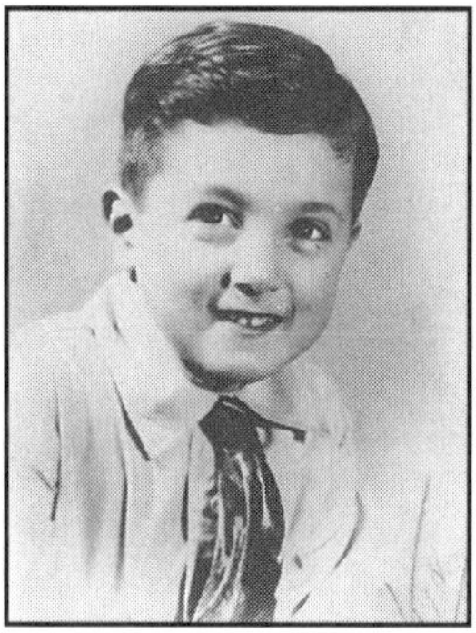

John at 6 years old

I was never allowed to come home late when I went out in the evenings, so I would sleep at my friend's house and, after a long work day, go out until 4 or 5 AM. After all the dancing and drinking, I was back to work at 8:30 the next morning. And all that for the devil. Today Christians barely sit through a whole church service and the Lord has given them the power of the Holy Spirit.

The drink kept me going. Today the drink is still keeping me going. Only now I am drinking from the Lord's cup that never runs dry.

I'm 19 now and here comes John, the "Italian stallion," back into my life. I watch him drive back and forth in front of my beauty parlor every week because he only lives a few blocks away with his family. In those days you never had your own apartment unless you wanted your head split apart. But hey, we loved it–our lives revolved around our family.

Now, I was determined to keep myself pure after hearing all this talk about sex in the beauty parlor. Just watching all my friends reinforced my decision not to join this club, but not because I was moral. I was not going to spend my money on some shrink after I worked so hard for it. So I made up my mind and set up a roadblock when it came to bed invitations.

One day John came by the beauty parlor to see me. Finally, the day I had been waiting for all these years! He invited me out for coffee and asked me to go away with him on a weekend trip. I thought both guys and girls were going, so I invited all my girlfriends. You know that wasn't his plan, and you can imagine how that went over. I didn't see him again for another year.

Then a year later we met again and this time it was love. That began "the days of wine and roses." We dated for a year and a half.

Chapter 3

Husband and Wife

And then we married.

My God, the next 10 years would be a waking nightmare for me. John began to open 'after hours' clubs and the years were cruel and hard. It was during those years that I began to drink heavily. Sometimes John would take me to one of the clubs and sit me at a table in the corner with a drink and a candy bar. It didn't help when his friends, trying to get in good with the boss, would continue to send over drinks to me all night long.

But no matter how much I drank, it seemed that I was able to work even harder. It's amazing how the devil can drive you. I was certainly no laydown drunk.

These were no longer "the days of wine and roses." It was black eyes and blows. There were so many holes in my apartment walls that I didn't have enough pictures to cover them. I would have had to hire Leonardo Da Vinci to paint the place. But I still played the picture perfect wife and the best cook around. That seemed to be the only thing that kept John married to me. But it didn't keep him home. (I am still feeding him, but with the Bread of Life as well. Wow! It really works!)

For five years I did everything you could possibly think of–and some things you would never dream of–to keep my husband home. I was determined to keep him. I changed my hair color so many times that my brain was losing lines from all the dye. No matter what color my hair was, no matter how long or short my hair was, and no matter what I wore to please and entice him, John's eyes were sealed for destruction. But God knew our destiny.

When changing myself didn't change him, I resorted to aggravating him. I remember all those times when John didn't come home at all, but went to his clubs all night. I always had to find a way to get even. I knew there was no way of winning, but it was always worth a try.

I would watch each night as John lay out his clothes on the bed and got ready to go out, knowing that he was leaving me home alone again. John was an impeccable dresser and he knew it. One night as he walked out the door, I went to the bedroom window to watch him walk by. He stopped, looked up at me with a smile on his face, and said, "How do I look?" There he stood, all decked out with his little Mafia hat on. I couldn't help myself. I called, "Wait!" Our apartment was on the third floor. I ran into the closet, grabbed all John's expensive suits, and threw them out the window at him!

For a minute I was caught up in watching him run back and forth, trying to save his clothes from hitting the pavement. Then I heard him say, "I'm coming to kill you!" I hurried to the coat closet and managed to pull myself up to the hat shelf. I could just barely fit, lying flat on my back, and I went as far back from the front of the shelf as I could get. I was thin and I was thankful that God had made short Italians, because when John opened the closet door, his head was far below the shelf I was hiding on, and he never saw me.

Our Wedding 1963

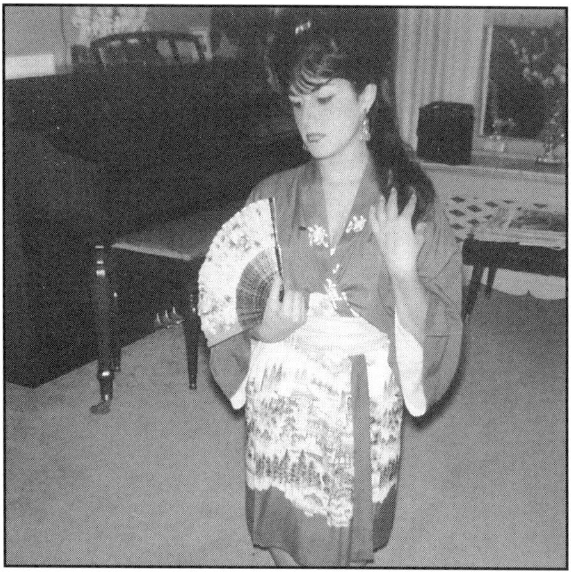

Marie at 21 trying a new look

Besides aggravating him, I also tried to give him the shock treatment. Once, in desperation, I pulled off the handle of a butcher knife, made a hole in my pajamas and taped the handle to my stomach. I put catsup all over to look like I had been stabbed. I put white powder on my face to try and look like I had been dead a long time.

I waited up until I heard the front door open. I threw myself across the bed with my head nearly touching the floor and my tongue hanging out, trying not to breathe and trying to look very dead. I really thought John's heart would break when he saw me. Surely this time he would be sorry for how badly he treated me and he would finally realize how much he loved me!

John came into the bedroom, looked at me lying there and said, "Do you have any hamburgers for all the catsup?"

Another night I was so angry, all I could think of was doing something that would really draw his attention to me. So I decided to make believe that I had killed myself. When I heard John open the front door, I went into the bathroom and locked the door. Then I threw a whole bottle of aspirin down the toilet, flushed it, and fell to the floor.

When John saw I wasn't in bed and that the bathroom door was locked, he immediately broke down the door. There I was, lying in a heap with the empty aspirin bottle by my side.

It was great. I got about a minute of his attention until he noticed the toilet. My little charade had backfired. The aspirins had floated back up and were fizzing and bubbling in the bowl.

John said, “I think the toilet just committed suicide” and walked out of the bathroom.

There was no end to the things I would do to try to keep John home, but to no avail. It was “Home Alone,” parts one, two and three.

Chapter 4

Orfanello & The Apple of My Eye

Very soon after we were married, I bought a beautiful statue of a little boy with golden hair, with a cup in one hand and an apple in another. The statue sat on a tall marble pedestal. There was writing on the bottom of the statue and for seven years, I thought it was just the name of the man who had sculpted it. (Remind me later to tell you the most incredible miracle concerning this statue!)

From the moment I married, I said that I would never have a baby of my own. I would always tell my husband, "Some day we'll adopt a little boy and his name shall be called John." John thought I was crazy and would tell me that even if we did have to adopt a child, he wanted a girl. We tried for years to have a child of our own, but without success. My words were true.

For these first five years of marriage, I had secretly saved all my tips from the beauty shop that I had worked so hard for. John always spent every nickel and dime we had on drinking and women. My little stash was just enough for a down payment on a house. So we decided to buy a home in New Jersey–a huge, beautiful home on one and a half acres of property for $33,000. I thought it was a dream come true, but it was only a continuation of the nightmare.

At first I thought that being so far from the city would help. But John had become a New York City fireman and one of the finest. That was to be expected. Anything he did, he went all the way. He was an incredible fireman. God was getting him ready to start fires in the hearts of men. However, the worst years were ahead of me and I became lonelier than ever.

After seven years of waiting to hear from the adoption agency, the call finally came while I was all alone. My husband was at work and on a fire call. The lady from the agency said, "Mrs. Sorrentino, we have a little boy with golden hair and skin as white as snow." She had just described my statue! There he was waiting for me, the apple of my eye!

Then I remembered how in years past back in New York when I had been so drunk, I would talk to my statue and say, "One day I am going to have a little boy and he is going to have golden hair just like you." Of course we were two dark–haired Italians, so the chances certainly were less than slim that we would have a child with blonde hair.

Three days later we were to pick up our baby, and we had nothing ready for him. Everyone else had nine months to prepare for their babies. In those three short days I was given two baby showers and I received 67 outfits from my co–workers and customers at the beauty parlor.

For years I could not figure out how to get rid of a coveting spirit that came over me when I saw others with children. Then I began to give baby showers with expensive gifts for my friends and family who were expecting and I would wait on them hand and foot after they had their babies, washing their clothes and cooking for them. You see, God did not say that the spiritual principle of reaping what we sow is only for Christians. It is for everyone in this life. I didn't yet know this wonderful God Who so loves to give to those who ask. But payday had come.

Our special day arrived and we picked up little John–John, only five days old. Life certainly changed, but my drinking did not. I thank God that I never neglected this child for even an hour.

One day a friend from Italy came to visit me. When she walked in, she saw the statue and said, "I just got the chills when I saw the insignia on the bottom of that statue." I replied, "Why? It's only the guy's name who made it." She said, "No, it's not! It's written in Italian and it says, 'ORFANELLO,' which means 'orphan boy.'"

I was amazed, but God was not, because He knew that statue would one day be sitting in my orphanage, surrounded by many orphan children. Nothing just happens! For the next three years, the drinking parties were getting worse and our fights more intense. We had graduated from the Brooklyn frying pan into a New Jersey oven, just one hour away. The devil was on a rampage to cook these two fish. But God–I said, BUT GOD–had the intention of adding the Bread and multiplying it.

There is so much I am leaving out, because this book would be the size of a dictionary if I included everything. But God will turn your trials into a trail that, if you take the straight and narrow path, will lead you to life.

Baby John at 3 months old

We got divorced a million times, but we never signed the papers. I murdered John in my mind and I would have done three life sentences. But the Son was soon to break through. Judge Jesus was getting ready to unlock my prison doors. The drunk that I had been for the past eight years would soon taste a new drink.

We came to the end of our rope and decided that moving back to New York might help, so we bought a beautiful house in Staten Island. Downstairs was a $5,000 wall–to–wall bar, an alcoholic's dream. But little did I know that it would be my burning bush.

We had been living in Staten Island for about three months when I came over the bridge from Brooklyn one day and saw my first rainbow. It covered the bridge from one end to the other. I said to my husband, "I feel like I am going through to a brand new life." I had no idea about Noah or about the covenant blessing.

CHAPTER 5

The Woman at the Well

One night after a severe drinking binge, my life would be forever changed. This night seemed like the worst drunk I ever had. My husband had taken my son, who was now three years old, and said he wasn't coming back. His leaving was not something new, but he had never taken my son before. I remember dragging myself upstairs to the balcony. I began to scream from my heart to God. As I did, it began to rain just enough to sober me up a little, just enough to find my way back into the house. I went downstairs to have another drink.

We had bookcases with tons of books on them. I had never read a book–I never had the time–but they looked good on the shelves. The week before, someone who didn't even know Christ herself had given me a little paperback Bible and I had carelessly thrown it up on a bookshelf.

I started to think of my son. I knew I had a family curse in my history. My father's brothers were all alcoholics. The curse had jumped over my father and landed on me. I had said I didn't ever want my son to grow up with a mother who was this way, so I decided to take my life.

Just before I did, I cried out one last time, "God, if You are real, I don't need You for my last rites, but I need You now! Reveal Yourself to me!" All of a sudden deep inside me I felt this impression to grab that little paperback Bible.

I opened it up and as I looked down, I couldn't believe it! But there it was! My eyes turned right to John 6:35 where it says, "I am the Bread of Life. He that comes to Me shall never hunger, and he who believes in Me, shall never thirst." I said, "God, You mean I'll never thirst for booze again? Lord, I believe!" At that moment I was totally set free!

I fell asleep and when I woke up, I had cried until all my mascara covered the page I had read, confirming that it was not a dream after all. Of course, the first thing I thought of was getting a drink, but when I went over to the bar, I found that the need for a drink was gone. My desire for a 'new drink' had taken its place.

God had chosen the perfect verse for me. No other scripture would have jumped out of the page like this one. "I am the Bread of Life" was for this Italian who was moved by eating, and "you'll never thirst" was for the drunk who was always thirsty. What a God! What a God!

Chapter 6

Born Again

Now begins my journey with the man who comes home to a born again believer who didn't even know she was born again. My life was transformed. My clothes changed, my tongue changed, and my sadness was turned to gladness. What a God! What a God! No one had to tell me that my skirts were too short or my blouses were too revealing. And I didn't even want to curse again.

So how do I prove this change to Mr. Macho Man? I didn't have to. My life was the living proof. I told John, "I'll never drink again!" His response was, "Sure, sure! I've heard that before!"

As I've shared with you, John had led me to drinking because of all the clubs that he had in the past. But now I was dancing with a new Partner. I now entered into revelation knowledge–a girl who never read a book now could not put down the Book of Books.

I began to ask God a million questions. I would just open my Bible and He would immediately answer me. I know, I know! You're not supposed to do that, but it was not yet grown–up time for me. Papa God was hand–feeding me. I was longing for answers, but I wasn't yet prepared to dig for food. His gentle hands were leading me step by step. What a God! What a God!

I wasn't getting much housework done. I was still working, but every spare minute was spent reading my Bible. I had acquired a hunger for my "new drink" and it more than satisfied me.

I could write a book alone from the events of the next six months. John began to come against me with everything he had. He told me, "All you do is sing and smile. You don't curse anymore. You're a nut! I'd rather have you drunk again! You were more fun."

I remember one particular day when John was sitting in our den with his feet up, drinking and watching television. Suddenly he began to tear me apart with his words. I went into our bedroom and said, "Lord, he's persecuting me!" I opened my Bible, and looking down, I saw the words of Jesus, "When they persecute you for My Name's sake, leap for joy." So I went back out into the den and obeyed Jesus. I began leaping all over the room right in front him. When he asked me what I was doing, I told him that Jesus had told me to do it. He wanted to order me a straightjacket! Not necessary! I was already on the straight and narrow path to Christ–righteousness!

What a God! What a God we serve! Imagine the God of heaven and earth, the Creator of all things, Who would take time in this crazy world to say one word that changes destinies and lives in a moment!

I longed to find one person who loved Him as I did. I would beg Him every day, "Lord, just one person." But God had me in Arabia all alone, to teach and settle in me His Word which would build the foundation of my life. Life begins only when you find Life itself. Jesus said, "I am the Life."

Chapter 7

John's Turn

How do I jump over so much of those first four months to share with you what came next? I am not here to put you to sleep... if I am, please let me know. I remember when Saint Paul preached so long that the man fell out the window because he fell asleep. But that didn't stop Saint Paul. He went downstairs, laid on top of him, raised him from the dead, went up and ate (that was the Italian part of Saint Paul) and began to preach again until the break of day. Those men never wasted any time.

Now I want to tell you about the night I had waited and prayed for. It had to be the time and season ordained by God. John finally said, "Put that Bible down or I'm leaving!" I replied, "You have taken everything from me but you are not taking Jesus." He grabbed my little well–worn Bible out of my hands and threw it in my face. Then he walked out the door and down our driveway.

This was the first time I didn't hold on to his feet and beg him not to go, as he was dragging me behind him. Once I had even jumped on the hood of the car as he was driving away, trying to hold on to him as I held on to the windshield wipers until I fell off. This time I stayed downstairs, holding the feet of Jesus.

John had purposed in his heart to go out and sin that night. But Jesus had a plan to clean him up. A man who had not cried since he was little was suddenly thrown down on the driveway and began crying like a baby. He felt God's hands upon his shoulders. As John began to scream, God verbally spoke to him. He actually heard God's audible voice say, "Go back." And while John was on his face weeping, God dealt with every area of his life, showing him His mercy and forgiveness.

John dragged himself back into the house, still dazed by what had happened. He began to choke me, saying, "You are making voices happen outside!" All I could say was, "John, it's Jesus. It's Jesus!"

Then he asked me what faith was. I told him that I wasn't sure what it was, but it sure felt good! I told him I would get on my knees and ask Jesus. I handed John my Bible and said, "Open it and He will tell you what faith is!" He replied, "I am too smart for that!" I begged him to just open the Bible and he finally did, opening to Hebrews 11:6, "But without faith it is impossible to please Him: for he that cometh to God must believe that He is, and that He is a rewarder of them that diligently seek Him." (KJV)

John asked me, "How did this happen?" and again, my only answer could be, "It's Jesus!" And then the words I longed to hear, "Okay, I am going to serve this God of yours!"

To God alone be the glory for the transformation which took place in the following six months.

CHAPTER 8

Our Honeymoon With Jesus

Through the years, John had been shot at so many times. Before we were married, he came home about 2 o'clock in the morning from a date. He parked his car in front of his parents' house and as he was walking to the door, a car drove by–spraying 23 bullets at him, with not one hitting him. Another time a man shoved a pistol in John's side and pulled the trigger. The pistol jammed and he was able to get away before the man tried again.

But now Christ would shoot straight through his heart. One day not long after John's experience with Christ on our driveway, he was outside mowing the lawn. Suddenly this unrecognizable language started coming out of his mouth. We had not yet set foot inside a church, and my newly saved husband was already speaking in tongues!

John came into the house and said, "I started speaking this crazy language–do you want to hear it?" I told him that I remembered reading something about that in Acts, about people who were talking like that. I found the scriptures in my little Bible and shared them with him.

I was now very jealous because John seemed to be getting ahead of me. I wanted that experience so badly! A few weeks later as I was frying meatballs, tears of love and joy began to roll down my face and I started speaking in tongues myself! My meatballs were burned, but oh, the fire of God had set my life on a brand new course.

John and I had no experience with any church other than the Catholic church, even though we never attended. About six months after the Lord revealed Himself to me, we were invited to go to church with the girl who had given me that little paper Bible that had changed my life so dramatically. Again, God used her even though she was not a born again Christian herself.

She took us to Calvary Tabernacle in a run–down neighborhood of Brooklyn, New York. As we walked in, everyone was praying in tongues. John said, "Listen! They're speaking our language!"

This was a great church with a great pastor, Dr. Benjamin Crandall, and here we planted ourselves, taking root and growing in the things of the Lord. For eight years John and I served at Calvary Tabernacle, from cleaning toilets to answering telephones–anything we were asked to do, we did with willing hearts.

What a God! What a God! Now John and I were really one. I didn't have to change my dress size or the color of my hair to keep him. Praise the Lord, God had become his Keeper.

I believe we personally spoke to our Pastor only four times during those years but we feasted on his messages. Pastor Crandall took the Word of God and brought us into the Bible to the point that you actually became like the saints who walked in those times. They were life–changing words. Today they need you to breast feed them every minute. Even when you pour yourself out to them, they say that God is leading them to a different church. Then in a year you find out that they have left that church, too. Ever learning but never coming to the truth, just as God said.

When Pastor Crandall preached, it was a confirmation of what God had already given us during the week as we sought His face. There was a certain phrase that really stood out when he spoke–"DON'T DO-O-O-O-O-O THAT!" It seemed like a paragraph, not a short sentence. And when you went home, you didn't do that!

And then he would use the word "fantastic." When Pastor Crandall said "fantastic," even if something didn't look good to you, that positive "FANTASTIC!" under the anointing of God was more than fantastic, it was dynamic!

We would listen to Pastor Crandall's life stories of faith over and over and every time it seemed like the first time. Faith never grows old. It was standing room only in that church for every service. People would fight for seats morning and night. Today the television is their source of night life. Pastor Crandall's altar calls never seemed to end because there was always room for one more at the foot of the cross.

Pastor Crandall was truly a shepherd that watched over his sheep and he seldom left his pulpit. I thank God for him and his lovely wife, Jeanne, who stood by his side through life's tragedies and triumphs. When we began to pastor our own church, we found we could only give what had been imparted into our own lives. We could draw on eight wonderful years of impartation.

Chapter 9

Let the Poor Say, 'I am Rich!'

Our lives were truly changed for the better, but we were now totally broke! Without the shady dealings of the past, John's salary as a fireman was not enough.

I was a great hairdresser and made tons of money, but now I began to talk about Jesus all the time. Whether washing their hair, dying their hair, or teasing their hair, my clients always got a song of praise from me.

Remember...this was an Italian Catholic neighborhood. As far as these girls were concerned, I had changed my religion and lost my mind. So one by one, they would leave until I had no customers left. After 18 years of hairdressing, with a large clientele, now there was no one. I sat in my empty chair and watched my customers go to the other girls.

My faith was really being tested and toasted. But I was too in love with Jesus to be moved. We still lived in a huge, beautiful house but now we had to live one day at a time by faith.

At first we were able to witness to all our family and friends but then the great rejection began. But through all my tears, the Lord put a shield around me. For every sorrow, I would open the Word and there would be a scripture to heal me. I tell you there is power in His Word when it is mixed with faith in Him!

It was simply Jesus–morning, noon, and night. We turned our neighborhood upside down. I helped bridge the gap between neighbors who hadn't bothered with each other for years. I lived in the house in the middle and reached them through my constant love and giving to their children who played with my son. This was my harvest field. All were welcome in our home.

I no longer drove. While living in New Jersey, I had so many parking accidents and the main street of our town was only three blocks long. I remember once I was trying to back into a parking space near the corner. I misjudged the distance and backed into the stop sign. I was trying to be very careful so the sign was going down very slowly.

Not only did I not know I was knocking down the sign, I also didn't realize that I was doing this right in front of the police station. An officer was standing there watching me, absolutely speechless from disbelief.

Another time I went to pick up my son from school. The parking lot was not paved and was covered with patches of wild grass. It was a big lot and a large rock that had never been removed was never a problem to anyone–that is, until that day. Somehow I managed to drive over the rock, get the car stuck on the rock, and start a grass fire as I gunned the engine to try to get over the rock. So, I did New Jersey and the world a great justice by tearing up my driver's license.

Now not being able to drive was no problem because I would sit outside on the curb and wait for people to pass by to tell them about Jesus, whether they wanted to hear it or not. I was in the hugging business, and they couldn't pass me by without receiving one.

One day a young man came to my door to sell me a carpet cleaner. Of course I invited him in. I told him I would listen to him if he would then listen to me, because I wanted to tell him about a "cleaning product" he had never heard of. He did his presentation, dirtying a spot on my carpet and then cleaning it up. Then he asked me if I knew anything that could match that.

Match that? And then some! I proceeded to tell him about a God Who wanted to reason with him, Who wanted to turn his scarlet sins as white as snow. He cried in my arms as I shared the love of Jesus with him and sent him on his way–with something much better than a sale–and of course, with a big bag lunch for him to eat!

It was not unusual for my husband to return home from the firehouse to find someone sitting at our kitchen table, learning about the Jesus Who had saved my life and set me free. He would warn me about letting strangers in the house, but I was so in love with Jesus, I could only see souls hungry for what I had to share.

A few years had passed and everyone in the church said the honeymoon with Jesus would soon cool down a bit. But my love for Jesus just got stronger and stronger with every trial. My trials became my trail to victory.

Chapter 10

Our Foster Children

Now God began to lay on my heart to take in foster children. Our first child was named Grace, the worst case imaginable to a foster parent. She was supposed to be with us for just a week or two.

Grace was a bag lady's daughter. She came with a bloated stomach and a legion of demons. We did not know anything about casting out demons in those days. We were just thankful to be saved.

Little did I know that God was preparing my heart for the orphans. I would ask Him why He would send me such a hard case, and He would answer with, "You do not know now, but you will know hereafter." We were in God's college, training for our future calling in Christ. And Grace, our first foster child–the bag lady's daughter–so socially retarded, would be the child we would adopt as our own.

Now, my son wanted a brother. One day the telephone rang while I was home alone. I was told that the agency had two Jewish sisters who needed placement. I told them that I really wanted a boy, but the Holy Spirit quickened me and I agreed to take the two little girls.

Mom, Carolyn and me
with John, Grace, Cassie and Shonna

Steve and Vinny
with Grace

One hour later the agency pulled up with the saddest children I had ever seen. I greeted the girls by telling them they were welcome in the Name of Jesus and they began to cry. They had been praying that God would bring them to someone who loved Him. I told them they certainly came to the right house.

I couldn't believe what they told me! They had once gone to the very church we attended. I called my church to speak with one of the leaders who was Jewish and born again. She told me I didn't have to explain why I was calling. The girls' grandmother had attended our church for years. She had been praying all night for them to come to us after she heard we were willing to take in children. The chances of this happening in New York City were a million to one, but there they were! My son came home from school and saw the two girls, who were five and eight years old, and remembered the older girl from his Sunday School class.

Two very rebellious boys, Steve and Vinny, came to our house for just weekend care. We were told that no matter where they were placed, these boys would run away.

I remember showing them around our beautiful house, asking them if they would like staying with us. Both the boys answered at the same time, "Wow! Yea!" I replied, "Listen, kids. If you want to run away again, let me know. I'll save you time and drive you."

That was the beginning of their extended stay with us. They accepted Christ into their hearts soon after and they fit right into our family, especially with my son. He was tired of all girls and finally got his brothers.

Chapter 11

A Life of Simple Faith

I never compromised my children and I didn't stick them in front of a television set to entertain them. Instead, I tried hard to teach them total victory, even at their young age. Our house saw a miracle every day, pure faith in action. However, I didn't even recognize them as miracles because they seemed to happen so fast. I just knew that God had done it before and that He would do it again. Oh, for those mustard seed days again! When we get older, the seeds seem so much smaller and the breakthroughs we are praying for seem so much larger.

The nights we held a time of praise and worship with the children, we used pots and pans for music. The children would march all around the house, making a simple melody to Jesus. One night as we were gathered around our kitchen table, the Lord said, "I am going to fill these children." A wind blew around the table and all the children began to speak in tongues except Grace. (Later I will tell you of God's "Amazing" Grace!)

These were trying years but faith building ones, as I had to pray in every meal and every stitch of clothing we had. My faith was simple.

I remember when little Shonna, our five–year–old foster daughter, needed tennis shoes for school. We all stood around her and I lifted her foot up to the Lord. I prayed, "Jesus, we don't even know her shoe size but You do! And we thank You for Shonna's new tennis shoes."

Two days later my cousin called me. We had not heard from him for several years. He had heard that we were taking in children. His wife had purchased a pair of tennis shoes for his daughter and they did not fit her. When she went to return them, she had lost her receipt so the store would not take them back. He didn't know if they were a size we could use, but he was passing by our house soon and said he would bring them. I assured him that they were the right size for Shonna and that we had been waiting for them. And they were exactly her size!

Shonna ran all over the neighborhood telling everyone that Jesus gave her a new pair of shoes. She came up to the atheist on the block, whose brother was a Catholic priest, and told him, "Look what Jesus gave me!" When he told her that he didn't believe in Jesus, she told him, "But He loves you!"

Every day was a new miracle. Out of nowhere a bag would be left on our doorstep with exactly what was needed for that moment. It might have been a dress that just needed a little mending or a coat that needed buttons.

I remember being on my knees praying, "Lord, it's almost 5 o'clock and there is nothing to eat." I was a great Italian cook but I still needed something to work with. Just then the doorbell rang and there stood a boy from across the street. He said, "My mom asked me to give this to you. It's five pounds of scallops. My grandfather owns a fish store. We have too much and they will go bad. Can you use them?" Of course, I replied, "I certainly can!" I found a loaf of stale Italian bread in the cupboard for my bread crumbs and a clove of garlic in my refrigerator. I was in business! Praise God!

Day after day this would happen. Every day I would make the kids a small cake from a mix. Remember, my education was extremely limited. I had to memorize the instructions on the box because I had difficulty reading them.

One day the kid next door asked me for an egg. I went to the refrigerator and saw that I only had one egg left. I said, "Lord, I'm not giving away my last egg. I can use it to make a cake." God said, "Marie, give him your last egg and believe you are giving it to Me when you give it."

I didn't give in easily. I replied, "Lord, they have money, they have two cars and they can drive." But God said, "Give him your egg." I told that kid, "Hold this egg tightly and don't drop it! That's my last egg."

It seems the Lord loves working with the last and the littlest. It really shows the "bigness" of our God. The next day the doorbell rang. It was a man from our church who thought we might be able to use five–dozen brown Jersey eggs! I just stood there and cried!

But that's not all. Years later, a man from Los Angeles decided to donate 7,000 eggs a month to our orphanage. He's been doing that for four years now. That's 84,000 eggs per year–336,000 total eggs to date! I wonder how many chickens that took. I just love God's math! You can't out–give God!

I remember that my bras all had holes in them. I held the best one up one night and said, "Lord, I don't even know my size anymore. But you know." I wasn't in the business of ever telling anyone I had a need, not even my family. My trust was in God.

Two days later my mother came to visit with a box in her hand. She said, "I bought these and took the tags off. See if they fit you." I opened the box and there were six bras–just my size, of course!

We were growing in Christ. But we were also five payments behind on our mortgage. I know, they should have taken the house by then. The man from the bank called and I told my husband to tell him that God said, "Grant me grace." John told him just that and there was silence on the other end of the line. The man excused himself and said he needed to speak with his boss. When he came back to the telephone, grace was just what we received.

I took all our bills and placed them inside my Bible. A few days later, when my husband was mowing our lawn, a man passed by and asked if John would mow his lawn, since he did such a good job on his own. That was the start of many lawn care jobs. And by the end of that summer, we had made all those back mortgage payments.

No, the bills were not paid by magic and the money didn't drop down from heaven. But the opportunity to make the money came from the One Who made the heavens.

Now we needed a truck. John had been using the back seat of our car to haul his equipment. At the beginning of the month, John had been looking in the newspaper for a van. I told him, "Throw the paper away and stop looking–by the end of the month, God is going to give you one."

We had a prayer meeting and Bible study at our house every week and it kept growing in numbers. One night someone said, "I have a van and I don't need it. Does anyone here need a van?" By the 30th of that month, there came the van.

However, there was a problem. This was our church's old van which had been given to this brother. Now, the van's motor was destroyed. So my husband laid hands on it and prayed for it to be restored to working order. Not only did the motor start, John drove it off the lot and we used the van for two years.

"Old Betsy," our pet name for the van, was a miracle right from the start. Although it was kept in working order by prayer and cost us no money for repairs, it had no heater and there was a huge hole in the floorboard. We always joked that in case the brakes went out, we could stick our feet through the hole and stop the van like the Flintstones!

One night we were going to church in the van, which was packed full with our own family and others who needed a ride. John was driving 60 miles an hour on the Verrazano Narrows Bridge when a tire blew. John told us all to get on our knees and start praying. There was no stopping on a bridge and we were in danger. It was freezing cold and so terribly windy on that bridge and our prayers for safety were fervent.

All of a sudden the van leveled off, it began to pick up speed and before we knew it, we were traveling at 60 miles an hour again. We finally had to stop at a red light when we came off the bridge and a man in the car next to us leaned out his window and said, "Hey mister! Do you know you're riding on your rim? There's no tire at all!" Dear Doubting Thomas, how would you explain this?

About half a block from the church, the van suddenly dropped down on one side, so we pulled over and parked it. The house of God was more important and we didn't want to be late. Jesus would figure this one out.

By the time service was over that night it was very late and we remembered that we had to replace the tire before we could go home. We had no spare tire–and no money to buy one. Much to our delight, there was a brand new tire on that empty rim. No, it wasn't repaired by an angel. I'm sure one of the brothers was touched by our need and filled it. But it was a miracle just the same!

Many times we would pick up others who needed rides from all over Staten Island and bring them to church in "Old Betsy." We would have just enough gas to get there and home again but not enough money to pay the toll for the bridge. God was so pleased with our willingness to go long distances out of our way to bring a soul to church that He always saw to it that someone who had no idea of our need would slip us a love offering to cover the cost of the toll and gas besides. God knew that we would raid our son's piggy bank for gas money if we needed to.

People from all over came to our church by bus, train, and bike as much as possible because we didn't have a parking lot. We all took a big chance parking our cars on the nearby streets. Many came out and found their cars without tires, rims and various other car parts. This rat–infested neighborhood was the pits and not the Ritz. No one cared because during the services, even with your eyes closed, His glory blinded you. We had much favor with "Old Betsy" since she already looked like she had been stripped! Nobody touched her!

We used our faithful "Old Betsy" for two years. After that we gave the van to a brother in the church who used it for a year and a half and then sold our old van for $2,500!

We had no money for vacations. But one day I said, "God, I have $5.00. Could we go away, Lord?" Some of the dear brothers and sisters that we knew owned a boat and a motor home. We were invited to join them as they rented an island in upstate New York for the cost of $25.00.

The island was tiny and you had to get to it by boat and sleep in a tent. I was definitely not the tent type. I needed a pot and a stove to make my pasta. But it was an adventure and it would be fun for the children.

And it was a beautiful island. But that didn't make up for the one outhouse that was a long way from our tent. They connected a string from the tent to the outhouse so that if you had to go at night, you could hold the string and follow it. Of course, that did not work for me. There were critters all over the island and the nights were long.

We ate hot dogs until they were coming out of our noses. So, one day, I decided I had to make my pasta. They had brought along a big pot and a little Bunsen burner and it took all day for the water to boil. But we ate pasta that night, after I believed for it and everyone else said it couldn't be done. They were blessed because it is not my nature to withhold food, even from non–believers!

We went on that vacation by faith, since we split the cost with several other families. I only had the extra $5.00 set aside and $5.00 was exactly what it cost us!

One day the man next door told me he was going away and asked if we would water his tomato garden. He would be back in a month and we could eat whatever came up while he was gone because he didn't want it to go to waste and rot. I cannot tell you how many times I harvested tomatoes to make a sauce. And not only were there tomatoes, there were eggplant and zucchini aplenty.

When our neighbor came back, I thanked him for letting us eat his tomatoes, eggplant and zucchini. Astonished, he said that he had only planted tomatoes and he had never planted either eggplant or zucchini!

God spent these eight years proving to me that my cruse of oil and jar of meal would not run out. These were the testing years, but always tasting that the Lord was good.

CHAPTER 12

My Husband, the Fireman

John had many narrow escapes with death throughout his life with the Mafia and then with the Fire Department. He was a real hero, always going beyond the call of duty to save many lives in the ghettos of Brooklyn. His was an incredibly busy firehouse where they did 5,000 runs a year. Many times he ended up in the hospital from injuries or exhaustion but always with miracle after miracle of God's saving grace.

John injured his arm in one fire and they said it was a hairline fracture down his forearm. They wrapped it up and sent him home, telling him to come back in the morning so they could set it. I laid my hands on his arm and prayed, "Lord, we don't have time for this. By Your stripes he is healed!" The next morning John went back to the hospital for x–rays, which showed no injury. They couldn't believe it, but we did.

I remember one night while I was at church, the devil said he was going to kill my husband. I grabbed a few of the girls and really prayed through. When I called John at the fire house, they said he was at a three alarm fire at a supermarket. The fire was so intense that the inside of the building had totally turned black with smoke and he could no longer see. He called out to God and just at that moment, light from the moon came through the skylight and led to an exit out of the building. Everyone who followed him was saved. That night John was breathing his last breath before God made a way. So many times this would happen, but God was always there to pull him out.

One day I remember John came home from a fire at a big food store. After putting out the blaze, the firemen had taken things to eat from off the shelves and out of the coolers. John loved rice pudding and there was a big tray of it, unharmed and ready for the taking. The firemen urged him to eat some, knowing how much he loved rice pudding, but he refused. That was the old man and this new man would not take something that he did not pay for. The firemen all laughed at him. John used to be the rabble rouser of the firehouse for years but now they called him "Father John."

He suffered tremendous persecution from these guys, but John stood his ground. There was no turning back for him. Later on through the years, John's steadfast spirit in Christ would pay off. They knew he was genuine and the men would secretly ask for prayer.

The next day after the rice pudding incident, the doorbell rang at home and there stood a sister in Christ. She had no idea what had happened but the Lord had prompted her to make a big tray of rice pudding and bring it to John!

Chapter 13

My Husband, the Disabled Fireman

In 1979, John was injured in an explosion in a fire. Several vertebrae in his back were severely damaged and eleven doctors agreed that an operation was necessary.

However, the Great Physician had another plan. The Lord had told me that no knife should touch his back. We believe that God uses doctors, but I also knew what God was saying to me. John and I believe in agreement and if I wasn't in agreement, he wouldn't submit to the operation.

The next year would be one of agonizing pain for him. He needed to walk with a cane, and one leg dragged. But we stood on my word from the Lord.

One day we were leaving the supermarket with John pushing the shopping cart, leaning on it for support. Again he heard that Voice loud and clear, the same Voice he had heard that day on our driveway when he got saved.

The Lord said to him, "John, if I heal you, what will you do with your life?" I didn't hear the Lord, of course, but I heard John say, "I'll serve You, Lord."

I asked him what he was talking about and when he told me, I was in awe that once again he had a direct word from the Lord. However, I thought his was a strange answer, since serving the Lord was what John was doing. But God was calling him to a greater service. Jesus was asking us to sell all and follow Him.

At this time we were leaders in the youth ministry of our church. A retreat was planned for February up in the mountains. At this retreat the Lord began to show me Psalm 149 and 150 and how to praise Him in the dance.

We had been in the middle of a revival at our church for years and didn't even know it. Hundreds were coming to the Lord and the youth group had grown from a handful to 600 in just a year. Even though it was a tongue–talking, fired–up church, we had never experienced the ministry of dance.

On the last night of the retreat, John was sitting on the altar with his feet hanging off the side. As his hands were lifted as he worshiped God, all of a sudden a warm feeling began to rush down his back. He leaped off the altar and began to dance before the Lord. Seeing John dance, we all began dancing. It was wonderful! What a miracle! John was totally healed that night by the power of God. Little did I know what was in store to follow this miracle.

CHAPTER 14

The Tent Meeting

Six months later we were invited to attend a Morris Cerullo tent meeting in Staten Island. We caught the last half hour of the event, but we saw enough to know that we had never seen anything like this meeting before. We had never seen the lame walk and the blind see before but we saw many healings that evening. And this night would impact our destiny forever.

As we were leaving the tent, we passed by a table filled with information on a school of ministry in San Diego, California. Before you know it, that flyer was in my husband's hand. I took it away from him and said, "Don't even look at that." I threw it on the floor. But I didn't know that as I walked out ahead of him, John picked up the brochure again and put it in his Bible.

John began a two week fast and I didn't know why. He was praying and believing that God would open my heart for us to attend this school of ministry in San Diego. Remember, I was Italian and very steadfast in my commitment to my life just the way it was. There was no way that I would move from my beloved New York, with all my family, my friends, my church and the food that I loved so dearly there.

John knew that it would take an act of God to change my heart and that was very true. He didn't share with me the reason for his fast, but I was about to find out in the most extraordinary way.

One day we were driving down a bad street in Staten Island. It was a rainy day. All of a sudden I began to see palm trees! I shook my head and rubbed my eyes but they were still there. I told John what I was seeing and he immediately began speaking in tongues, praising God and crying so hard he had to pull the car over to the curb.

I asked him why he was crying and he explained that the palm trees meant California. I told him he was crazy. He then told me he had been fasting because only God could change my stubborn Italian heart. I assured him that it would take more than a vision of palm trees to change my mind. He was not deterred and told me to go ahead and put fleeces before the Lord–God always answered me that way. Didn't I love God and want to follow Him, he asked? My faith had been challenged many times but no one had ever challenged my love for God.

So I went home, determined to choose some really difficult fleeces to put before the Lord. I really wasn't worried because I could not conceive that God would ever ask me to leave New York.

First of all, we still had all the foster kids and Grace. Even though we were trying to adopt her, we could never go to another state legally with her. Secondly, our beautiful house had been on the market for years with no buyers. It seemed we couldn't even give it away. Finally, there was that 100 year–old tree just past my back yard in a land reserve. It, and all the other trees on the reserve, had obstructed what would have been an incredible view from my floor to ceiling window at the back of my house. No one would ever build there because it was a reserve and the trees were protected.

There they were–three impossible fleeces. I felt very secure, believing that my husband would get over this crazy idea of moving to California.

The very next morning as I was praying in my favorite spot by the window in the back of the house, I heard a big noise outside. As I looked out of the window, I saw a bulldozer not only taking down that 100 year–old tree but every tree on that reserve! Someone had gotten the zoning changed and was going to build a house there. Then I knew that God was beginning to build my house where He lived–in my heart.

My husband ran into the room when he heard the noise of the bulldozer and he couldn't believe his eyes. He said, "God really has a sense of humor with you! Do you believe Him now?" I replied, "He has two more fleeces to go!"

A week later we had to go to court for Grace. We had gone many times before but Grace was not adoptable. Grace's birth mother could have her back if she would clean up her garbage and make a suitable home for her daughter. But Grace was part of this bag lady's garbage and she was not going to let go of her and give her to me. But still we kept trying.

We arrived at the proper courtroom only to find out that the case had been the day before! But I was sure that I had remembered the correct date. We called the social worker, who asked us who we knew that worked on our behalf. There was no way we could win our case without being there, yet we did win! We had permission to take Grace to California if we wanted to. She was released to us and ready to be adopted. God was our counselor that day! He definitely showed up, even if we didn't.

Two down and one to go. I was amazed at the miracles that were happening to us but chose not to associate them with a move to California. After all, there was still our house and I was still looking at Hotel Jonah.

When we got home from court there was a couple standing on our lawn. He was a lawyer and had brought his wife to look at the house, which we had recently taken off the market. His words were few, but to the point–"We want to buy your home."

Chapter 15

Off to California

We began to pack and everyone thought we were crazy. I did too, and my heart was breaking, but I had put my own fleeces before the Lord and He had answered every one in record time. What else could I do?

My father and mother would be left with my sister who was afflicted with MS plus the scoliosis of her spine. She was twisted, deformed and bedridden now. My heart broke to leave her. The church I loved and had been active and productive in for the past eight years would become only a memory.

Life would no longer be the same. With great decisions come great costs. There are no cheap goods in God's Kingdom. God gave the best when He gave His Son. And what about the little girls and the two boys?

One night God woke me up and told me He would be returning the two girls, Cassie and Shonna, to their mother. I couldn't believe it. I had grown to love them so much, I thought it would be impossible to let them go. I opened my Bible and looked down, seeing the passage where Solomon returned the child to the rightful mother after first saying he would cut the baby in half. I said, "No Lord, don't divide them."

The next day, just as the Lord had said, the authorities came to return the children to their mother, much to my great sorrow. The boys would be placed in other foster homes as well.

California, here we come–not by my choice but by my surrender. Like the Beverly Hillbillies from Brooklyn, we were on our way. We sold almost everything and those things we needed were stowed away in or on the roof of the motor home we purchased for the trip. We loaded up the dog, the cat, and the two kids. We had become like Abraham and Sarah. I cried all the way from Staten Island, New York to San Diego, California.

We had only planned to stay three months for the school of ministry, but I knew in my heart we were not coming back.

CHAPTER 16

New York versus California

Wilsie, "Miss Lines on the Brain," has just reminded me that I cannot leave out a lot of the goodies that have made her laugh and cry over the years. This would be a great time to tell you some things that might fill in the blanks.

When we moved to California, it was the greatest culture shock I have ever experienced. When the Lord made California, He tilted it to the side and everything from the other states fell down this way. It's a place where you do your thing. Everyone lives their own lives and yet they think they know the Lord.

California was certainly a far cry from what I was weaned on. And I am no legalist. I do shave my legs, wear pretty clothes, and my hair is real short. The Christ that led me always said, "If you lose your life, you will gain it." And that was not what I was seeing. In my 30 years of salvation, I never remember a time when someone was not living with us, someone for me to serve.

In Brooklyn, the backyards were so small you could have kissed someone on the other side without having to move, but there were always people there, cooking on the barbecue, eating, fellowshiping, gardening their little basil and tomato plants, hanging out their laundry and talking to the neighbors on what they planned to cook for dinner that evening. In California, every Taco Bell, McDonalds, and every other fast food place is packed for dinner, almost always with single parents.

I remember how I cried when we first came to California. I said, "Lord, I gave away and sold everything for you. But there must be a salami and mozzarella, ricotta, and provolone cheese in sight somewhere!" It was six months on the wagon without that wonderful smell that seemed to reek from the Italians.

Now don't misunderstand me. I became all things for the sake of the elect. There wasn't anything I wouldn't try to win a soul to Jesus. But that Martha part of me was crying out.

One day my husband went to play racquetball and I went along. I was bored so I told him I would just take a little walk around downtown while I waited for him. As I was walking, all of a sudden the smell of provolone–the real thing–came into my nostrils. I had no idea where that came from. I thought I had stepped into the "twilight zone." I looked up and over my head on a street light was a sign that read, "Little Italy." I followed my nose and walked into a store. I started speaking in tongues and crying. You name it–if it was Italian–it was there. The clerk said they shipped all their stuff here from Brooklyn! Proverbs 31 says that this lady went far for her food and that is what I began to do. Everyone benefitted from "Martha's Italian Kitchen."

The smell of food seemed to draw everyone. People would ring my doorbell saying, "Lady, what are you cooking? There is an incredibly delicious smell up the block, especially of garlic."

Chapter 17

The MCWE School of Ministry

The very first day we went to school, someone had tried to break into the house we had rented. My son, John, was now 11 and Grace was 10. They had been home alone. That was all it took for me. I insisted that I was taking the kids and going back to Brooklyn.

However, my son said, "No, you are not going home! You are going to be strong and finish school!" So I reluctantly remained, thanking God for my faithful German shepherd dog, Princess, who was a great watchdog over both the house and the kids.

John grew spiritually by leaps and bounds at the school. The anointing of Dr. Morris Cerullo had truly been passed on to him as well as to the other students. But John was overflowing with it. In fact, John even looked like him.

We continue to thank God for Brother Cerullo's life and his anointing, which has been transferred to so many. Truly our lives would never be the same.

As for me, I passed those three months sitting toward

the back, eating "Good and Plenty" candies and trying to stay awake.

The day of registration, we met four people we had known in New York who also came to attend the school of ministry. They had come by faith, standing in line to register with no money for tuition and no place to live.

We gave two of them the money for their tuition and took them home to stay with us. That was the beginning of the revolving door of my home that operated nonstop for the next twenty years.

One by one, people began to come from New York to visit and many stayed and never returned. However, not all who came through my door left with a happy ending.

Life in Christ is a matter of choice and choice definitely determines your destiny. Your love for Christ is not enjoyed by all. The Word says, "I'm a companion to all those that fear Thy Name and keep Thy precepts." So not all fear God. The Word also says that the fear of the Lord is the beginning of wisdom. So many begin by fearing Him but do not continue that way, so the wisdom departs and the wise become dumb.

I had asked my husband to not be noticed so that we could go home. By the time the school was over, John was not only the head usher but was also the valedictorian of this school of 750 students from all over. It was the most incredible group of people, with miraculous testimonies of how each one had come from every nation of the world to this school. So much for keeping a low profile.

Toward the end of the three-month session, the Lord woke me one night and told me that we would have three offers before school ended but He would tell me which one to accept.

One by one the offers came. The first one was to go to Africa to be missionaries. The second came a few weeks later, when we were invited to be assistant pastors of a church in Toronto, Canada.

The Lord woke me again one night and told me that John would be asked to stay on at the ministry as Chaplain of World Evangelism. This was the third offer and the one the Lord wanted us to accept. So I woke John up to tell him what the Lord had said about the last offer that was coming.

The next day Dr. Edwin Louis Cole, the head counselor and a great man of God, asked to see us after school. He brought us to the top of the El Cortez Hotel, which was the tallest building in San Diego at that time. The top floor was all glass with an incredible, panoramic view of the city. (Even then, God knew my desire for a beautiful view!) This huge area was filled with telephones so that people could call from all over the world to ask for prayer and counseling. Well, that did it–no more looking back to New York.

Chapter 18

The Ministry Years

The very same week we started working for the I CARE telephone ministry of Morris Cerullo World Evangelism, all the counselors quit! So for an entire year, we answered the telephones all day and then had the lines transferred to our home after the work day and we answered telephones all night!

After the year was up, my husband was asked to stay on as the North American crusade director for Morris Cerullo World Evangelism. Now it was time for the nightmare of my life to begin.

John traveled all over for the next five years. Remember, I no longer drove. We moved into an apartment complex and the battle began. My health was at an all–time low, and my partner was gone.

After two years had gone by, I fasted and prayed and the Lord spoke to me on the 20th day of my fast. He told me I would be traveling with my husband. I had never preached a day in my life and now the Lord was asking something of me that was far out of my range.

That day John called me and I told him what the Lord had said. My husband said I was crazy. Besides, there was no way we could afford that. I told him I knew that, but that is what the Lord said.

Two days later John called me back and said, "You won't believe it, but they want you on the field with me to help!" And that began another chapter in my life as we traveled all over together.

One day as I was sitting in the back of one of the churches, John called me forward to sit in the front row. When I got to the front, he called me to sit on the altar with him. When I sat on the altar, he asked me to say a few words.

I was so scared that I almost fainted. I stepped into the pulpit, which wrapped around and should have accommodated two people. However, John had put on some weight and we got stuck! We couldn't get out, and of course, everyone found that pretty funny. But it was our beginning and we ministered all over together after that.

Chapter 19

The Moving Altar

We were attending a local church during this time, but it was pretty dead and our kids, who were now teenagers, were backsliding. I had told my husband that if we didn't find a good church soon, I was going back to New York. It seems I wasn't sealed after all those years.

After five years on the field, as my husband was flying back from Denver, he was praying about the spiritual needs of our family. The voice of the Lord came to him again and told him to build a church. That was an answer to our prayer but not necessarily the one I was looking for.

We started with a Bible study in our home that began with eleven people, but rapidly grew each week. The neighbors would call the police on us all the time. We were those loud "Jesus freaks." When the policeman would come, I would tell him we were praying for him also. He would say "Thank you, but could you ask God a little more quietly?"

In order to prepare for these services, our house was turned upside down. The dining room table had to be put outside on the patio. My husband would preach on a box. People sat all the way up the stairs to the bedrooms. We would baptize in our pool in the back yard.

One day I was going to the bathroom and I was talking on the telephone. All of a sudden I heard someone else's voice on the phone, not the person I was talking to. I realized it was my neighbor's voice. I could hear her but she couldn't hear me. She was telling someone how she was going to get even with those "Jesus freaks" by calling the authorities and telling them we were operating as a church in our home. I couldn't believe my ears! The Lord had given me a hotline from Heaven to hear my enemy's plot, while I was sitting on the toilet!

My husband called the authorities himself. He asked if they would give us a month to find a new meeting place and they agreed. When my neighbor went to the authorities to expose us and complain, her plan exploded in her face. If God be for you, who can be against you?

From temporary place to temporary place, it was the same complaint–we were too loud and too in love with the Lord. We had named the church New Covenant Tabernacle, but at the time we didn't realize that "tabernacle" meant "moving altar" and that's exactly what we were.

I remember when we had a congregation of about 30 people and were meeting in a small room of a local Lions Club. We received a telephone call asking my husband to candidate for a church of 3,000 in another state. The church had its own elementary and high schools, there was a beautiful parsonage provided as a home to the pastors, and the salary was incredible.

The kids were all excited and so were we–until I asked what "color" the church was. When I was told that all the people were "white," I said, "Wrong church!" The Lord had promised me a Joseph's coat of many colors church. We sat on the bed and cried.

That night the Lord said to me, "Since when did you ever eat Ragu spaghetti sauce? Everything you cook is made from scratch and that's the way I'm building this work. No shortcuts allowed!"

My sauce takes hours to make so I knew this would be a long haul. Someone had told me that anything that grows too fast can become cancerous. I said, "Well, Lord, where you lead me I will follow. No cloud, no go. No fire by night, no rest. Two years and several temporary locations later, we finally found a place to put down roots and grow. It was an old movie theater which had last been used for pornographic movies. The first time we were shown the property we said we weren't interested. It had been empty for two years and the interior was destroyed. There were rats running around, inches of water that couldn't drain where the altar would have to be, and the seats were ripped and filthy. But we couldn't find anything that would work for us or that we could afford, and we felt the Lord leading us back to that vacant theater.

We tore the place up, and God helped us build a beautiful sanctuary that could seat 650 people.

Chapter 20

The Lily of the ValleyS

Two years later, in 1988, we were planning to televise our church services. The Lord spoke again and said now was the time for the Lily of the Valley.

Many years before as I was on my hands and knees, washing my kitchen floor under the table, the Lord spoke to my heart and said that one day I would have an orphanage. He led me to Isaiah 54:1, "Sing, O barren one, you who did not bear; break forth into singing and cry aloud, you who did not travail with child! For the [spiritual] children of the desolate one will be more than the children of the married wife, says the Lord."

I asked, "If this is true, Lord, what will I name it?" I went to my Bible and opened it up to Song of Solomon. 2:1, "I am the rose of Sharon, and the lily of the valleys." God said the orphanage would be called The Lily of the Valley.

I had carried that promise in my heart for years, waiting for the appointed time, but never realizing that this orphanage would be on foreign soil. God said now was the time, but the question was where?

That conversation with the Lord went like this. "But Lord, where do you want the orphanage? You know I hate Mexico." "Yes, Marie, and that is why I want you to have one there."

So the first Lily of the Valley Orphanage in Tijuana, Mexico, came into being and there went Orfanello, our little statue that we had since we were first married. When we left New York I had given the statue to my mother for safekeeping and now we could send for it.

The money we had set aside for television now went into remodeling a big house that we rented to use as an orphanage. Our church was more than generous. We were a family, pulling together to make it work. Then the Lord began to send the faithful workers–the live-in staff who are still there with us today.

Our first children came from Tijuana's garbage dump and prison. The dump was home to the city's poorest people, who lived in cardboard shacks and scavenged food from the piles of garbage. Many times the children were abandoned there, unable to care for themselves, and the neighbors were too poor to take them in.

In Mexico, families went to jail with whoever was sent there and they lived on the outskirts of the cells in miserable poverty. There was no place else for them to go. Many times children were born to mothers in jail.

These abandoned and rejected children told us the most horrible stories about the abuse they had suffered–they were raped, burned, beaten and scarred, both mentally and physically. But there was Jesus, just waiting to embrace them and fill them with His love. He truly is the Father of the fatherless.

Several years later the orphanage caught on fire one

night just before Christmas. The gate to the high walled fence surrounding the building was secured each night with a lock, and the key to that lock–and the only escape route–was inside the burning building.

All 41 of the children that were currently housed there, as well as the five staff members, got out of the building safely but the heat from the fire was threatening to explode the propane gas tank that was in the courtyard. It started to rain but not enough to even touch the flames that reached to the sky.

There was no one to help and no fire truck arrived for over an hour, but God sent His angel–or Jesus, Himself–to rescue them. A man came to the gate and told them not to be afraid. He reached out his hand to each child and each staff member and helped them climb over the courtyard fence. Afterward they said it was almost as if there was an invisible ladder for them to walk on because everyone held by his hand made it safely over the wall and was led to safety. When we went to thank him, he had disappeared.

It was 2 o'clock in the morning and we joined the children and staff, standing on the street in their pajamas, giving thanks to God for their safety, but freezing and weeping just the same. Where would these 46 people go in the middle of the night? All their belongings and all our resources had been destroyed by the fire.

Earlier in the evening we had gathered together to celebrate Christmas and the children had opened the gifts of toys and clothes that were so generously donated to them. How could these same children, who just hours before were joyously celebrating the birth of Christ, be homeless? And what could I do about it?

We knew that our church people would gladly house children and staff until we could find a permanent place for them, but the authorities we contacted that night refused permission to bring the children to the United States. And the government would not provide a place, even temporarily. We contacted some of the local churches who were close to the orphanage, but they refused to open their doors to us. Our emergency didn't happen during business hours.

In those early morning hours, we joined our tears and petitions as we asked God to help us. Just then, a young man from across the street came home from work late and stopped by to see what had happened. Immediately he invited us to bring all 41 children and the staff to his home. He was newly married, but he knew that his wife would agree. He apologized that his house was not very big, but all were welcome.

To us his home looked like a palace, even though the children had to be housed in one room. I remember saying that I would find a way to feed them. He told me not to worry since he owned a small restaurant and he had food enough for everyone.

Besides this dear couple, no one except our own church reached out to help. As the churches turned a deaf ear to our plight, I began to cry out to the Lord, Whose ear has always been open to my cry.

The next day the story hit the newspapers in both Mexico and San Diego. The headline called it 41 miracles. Before you know it, the story was on television. San Diego reporters were covering the aftermath of the fire from the orphanage, interviewing our staff and some of the children. Suddenly people began to come from all over with blankets, clothes and food. This was a long, hard hour but the Lord began to work out His plan.

The day following the fire, we found a real estate agent to help us locate a suitable place to rent. As she was checking out various places, the Lord spoke to her to give us her own home for a month and that is just what she did. Within that month, she found a place for us to locate. The children and the staff were excited to move in and began to make it home.

We stayed in this rented home for about a year. The night of the fire I had fainted because I was so overwhelmed. But in my spirit I heard the Lord say to me, "Greater than this shall you build." And that promise came to pass.

Out of this group of children, we had put together a choir of little angels who sang their hearts out for Jesus. Their singing was truly heavenly. A year after the fire, the children of the Lily of the Valley Orphanage were invited to sing at the Morris Cerullo World Evangelism world conference in Anaheim, California. At that conference, the Lord led Dr. Cerullo to take an offering for a permanent home for the children. Enough money was raised to buy a former cancer hospital in Tijuana for a permanent orphanage site.

Our church worked day and night to make this hospital a home for the children, a hospital for Jesus. As those unwanted, unloved children walked through the doors of this orphanage, the mighty power of God delivered and set them free, and filled them in and out with His love and His Holy Spirit.

We didn't have a lot of land, so being New Yorkers, we built things high. First we built our own school for kindergarten through sixth grade on top of the kitchen building. Soon every building added an upper floor as more and more children came to us.

Hundreds of children had come through the Lily of the Valley Orphanage. But I knew it had not ended, although I forgot that there is an "s" at the end of valleys in the verse God had given me. The Lord had more than one in store.

Seven years later the "s" appeared. We had been asked to fly out to Chihuahua, Mexico to look at a ranch property for another possible orphanage. This was 1,200 miles away from our first orphanage in Tijuana, and although I knew there would be others, I never expected to start another one in Mexico.

In the middle of the desert, with dead cows lying along the road, there sat a terribly run-down building. It looked like a depressed cowboy movie set, certainly not a place where Roy Rogers would have ridden. We had been asked to buy and take over this so-called orphanage which was presently home to five children.

By now the Lily of the Valley in Tijuana was rated the finest orphanage in all of Baja, Mexico. This was not just because of the nutritious, delicious food we served the children, but because of the love we gave them, and most of all, because of the Holy Ghost. The government was amazed at the current mental state of these children who they knew had been so battered, abused, and neglected. The government had so much to say in the placement of these children, but gave so little to their care and rehabilitation.

We knew we could do it again, but who would actually go to Chihuahua and take over? A couple, Ed and Rosa Salo who were both assistant pastors in our church for eight years, and whom we had trained, were willing to go there to live and be the parents to the children our new Lily of the Valley Orphanage II would house.

Lily of the Valley I

Lily of the Valley II

Again, the children of the Lily of the Valley choir in Tijuana sang their hearts out at a Morris Cerullo World Evangelism conference. And again, the Lord used Dr. Morris Cerullo to raise the $25,000 necessary to buy the property in Chihuahua.

That seed began to multiply. The children at the Chihuahua orphanage began to pray and fast. Soon unbelieving businessmen came to fill the needs at the Lily of the Valley II and began to build for us. About $500,000 has been spent as they built a huge beautiful kitchen, new dormitories for the boys and girls, and a fence around the entire property. God certainly knows how to stretch a dollar.

Chapter 21

John & Grace

After we had been pastoring New Covenant Tabernacle for seven years, my son, John–the apple of my eye–left home and backslid. The Lord had begun to remind me of all the promises He had given me concerning my son. He told me John would be pastoring beside my husband one day. I seemed to have lost everything except for God's promise for the prodigal. After nine months of travail, I finally gave birth. My son, John, returned, married.

Three and a half years later we were sitting at my table eating when I jumped up and said to my son, "Are you ready for what God has for you?" Such a surge of faith had hit me. Usually he would say, "Mom, please stop!" His dream was to be a lawyer. This time he didn't give his usual answer.

Two weeks later, my son, John, went on staff as New Covenant Tabernacle's youth pastor. God's promise had again come to pass. What a God! What a God!

John and his wife, Jackie, have a son named Giovanni, the second apple of my eye. They had been married seven years in 1999, when they found out they were expecting a child. They were sure the baby would be a girl. But I went to Jesus and He told me that the baby would be a boy with blond hair and blue eyes–a 'white as snow' baby. On October 14th of that year, who came forth but a baby boy, who looked like John's twin.

Giovanni is the most affectionate child I have ever known, bestowing kiss after kiss to his very willing grandmother. It's like reliving the years with my son.

There is a part of me that will always be a child. It seems kids are drawn to like spirits. Jesus wants us to be childlike, not childish.

One of our biggest miracles has been our daughter, Grace, the child we adopted at seven years old and our most impossible case. Grace joined the Navy right out of high school and was stationed on the East Coast. Sadly to say, Grace never found the Lord for herself in all those years with us, although she saw Him move mightily time and time again.

Grace married and had a beautiful little girl named Katrina. Our precious granddaughter came to live with me and her Grampa for a month when she was five years old. We took her to Sea World, Disneyland, and the world-famous San Diego Zoo but she was not impressed until Sunday when she walked into our church for our annual Christmas cantata. Worship had begun after the presentation of Christ's birth, life, death, and resurrection had been so beautifully portrayed. Katrina started to cry uncontrollably, saying, "Grandma, Jesus really loves me." I replied, "Yes, He does, my little one." Immediately she was filled with the Holy Spirit.

Katrina continued to cry and when we arrived home, she wanted to talk to her mother on the telephone. When Grace answered the telephone, Katrina said, "Mommy, Jesus died for us and loves us." Grace answered with, "I know, I know." But really, in her heart, she didn't know.

The Word of God says that a child shall lead them. Katrina went home from her vacation an on–fire five year old, turned loose on her mother. Katrina spoke of Jesus all the time and begged her mother to take her to church. The Lord arranged for person after person to tell Grace about Jesus. There was only one escape, and that was into the arms of Jesus. He had been waiting for such a time as this. It didn't take very long after that for Grace to receive Jesus Christ as her personal Lord and Savior.

Grace bought a home in Virginia on a street called Bonita Drive. Bonita, California was the place where she grew up. And she now attends a church called New Covenant Church, almost the same as ours!

See, you can keep walking away from God but you will only walk around in circles. Bless God, you'll meet Him where you left off. Jesus was a mountain climber. He never went around the mountain. It may be a long way up, but you would not believe how strong your legs become. So then Jesus says when your brother asks you to go an extra mile, you've already had your training.

John Jr. with John Sr. at 2 years old

John Jr. with Giovanni at 2 years old

Jackie, John & Giovanni

Katrina

Grace & Family

Chapter 22

Until Part 2

There are many churches that support orphans. However, I don't know of a single church that owns their own orphanage and whose pastors run it and also pastor the church. When I think of the years past, I know why the Lord doesn't tell you too much of the future. Remember the scripture He would always give me? It was John 13, verse 7, "You know not now ... but you will know hereafter." In plain English, He is saying "Mind your own business. You couldn't handle all that I am about to do."

We have been at our theater–turned–church for about 16 years now. Here we sit, in the middle of this crazy strip mall. There is a bar to the left, providing drunks to urinate on our cars. On the other side of the bar is a laundromat where you can be sure your clothes will be stolen if you don't stay there and watch them. On the right side of the church, there is a supermarket which has already changed hands three times. Next to the market is a liquor store that has been held up frequently.

Drug addicts, alcoholics, street people–you name them! They have passed by and entered into this church.

According to our statistics, without evangelistically stretching the truth, over 10,000 people have passed through the doors of New Covenant Tabernacle.

Cars have been stolen and our children have run around in the parking lot and it has been only by the grace of God that they have not been killed. There is definitely an invisible sign on the front of this church that says, "Children Welcome," because every time I look, there is another child! My husband has asked the congregation not to drink from the water fountain in our lobby. We think that the Lord has blessed that water with fertility! In the midst of all of this craziness, I love it just because I know that the King feels comfortable here. And where He is, that's where I am also.

You know I am going to have to write part two of Plain Vanilla Jesus because at age 61, it seems as if it is just beginning. I know there are more orphanages to be built. We have purchased 10 acres of land, but the church has not yet broken ground on the new building. Already from this mother church, three more churches have sprung up in the poorest areas of Tijuana, Mexico, with three of our Elders pastoring them.

A rocking chair sounds great, but the Rock of All Ages is far greater in my life. So this old battle axe has yet a lot more trees to cut down and so much more can be built up.

More flavors than plain vanilla have been added through the years. At times it seems so confusing which to choose. But my eyes always seem to stick to vanilla.

Maybe you are reading this book and saying, "Can God use me?" Hey, don't tell anyone, but He created you to use you! You are a large part of His plan. But you'll never know His plan until you erase your own. Jesus said in

Jeremiah 29:11, *"I know the thoughts and plans that I have for you, says the Lord, thoughts and plans for welfare and peace and not for evil, to give you hope in your final outcome."*

I've learned that the Potter likes to cook, too. He makes us tender as we remain cooking real slow. I know my meat tastes great. And that's what we are–meat for a hungry world. The problem is that sometimes meat is tough and you have to spit it out because there is no way to digest tough meat.

I pound my meat with a wooden hammer to tenderize it. Being that meat would be no fun, but just taste how delicious it is afterward. So, the pounding of your life is not there to break you, but to make you fine tasting.

Never remember what you give, but always remember to keep thanking Him for what you get. Then you are a real giver and a candidate for the Lord to give to you more than you could ever expect.

Your hands are God's plans. So give Him your hands and He will meet you with His nail-scarred hands and the two of you will become one to be directed by Him.

The Lord may have to tear up a few pages of your life. Don't worry. You won't miss them anyway.

I thank the Lord that He covered my eyes. It truly has been a surprise party all these years.

John & Marie
Celebrating 40 years of Marriage

Dear Reader,

Do you feel something–or Someone–is missing in your life? Have you tried unsuccessfully to find that missing puzzle piece? I can help.

Won't you say this prayer with me? Come on, it only takes a moment and it really, really works if you say it from your heart.

"Lord, I'm not going one more minute until You come into my heart and become Lord. Forgive me for my failures, my sins. Wash me with Your precious blood and forgive me. Thank You for the gift of eternal life. Father, thank You for sending Jesus to me to make a way. I pray this prayer in Jesus' Name. Amen!"

Welcome to the Kingdom, my Brothers and Sisters. I didn't want to leave without you and I'm so glad you decided to come along. It's free to you, but paid for by the costly blood of Jesus–because He loves you!

His Handmaiden,

Marie

P.S. Remember to look for a copy of *Consider the Lilys, How They Grow*, my next book! It will contain some of the most incredible stories and pictures of the children brought to our orphanages over the last 15 years. After reading these horror stories that turned "garbage" to "glory," you will never be the same!

ABOUT THE AUTHOR

Born and raised in Brooklyn, New York, Pastor Marie Sorrentino came to San Diego, California, with her husband, John, a former New York City Fireman, to attend the Morris Cerullo School of Ministry. God called them to full-time ministry and they pioneered New Covenant Tabernacle Church in 1985.

She and her husband founded the Lily of the Valley Orphanages in Tijuana and Chihuahua, Mexico, fulfilling God's promise to her while scrubbing her kitchen floor many years ago. These are now home to over 200 children who have been rescued from the garbage dumps, streets and prisons of Mexico.

Pastor Marie ministers to the Body of Christ on marriage and relationships, mentoring, servanthood, and leadership. She shares her dynamic testimony of how God delivered her from eight years of alcoholism, her husband from the Mafia, and God's faithfulness to her over the years.

Please feel free to share your thoughts with Pastor Marie at:

Email
plainvanillajesus@yahoo.com

Mail
Lily of the Valley Orphanages
P.O. Box 1108
National City, CA 91950